Lire à petits pas Niveau

Méthode Montessori pour apprendre à lire : du mot au livre

French English German Spanish - Portuguese

girl   fille

fille

niña   menina

The girl is pretty.

---

floor   sol

sol

suelo   chão

The girl sits on the floor.

---

house   maison

maison

casa   casa

We live in the same house.

hoe — houe

houe

azada — enxada

Use a hoe in the garden.

idea — idée

idée

idea — idéia

I have an idea!

cotton — coton

coton

algodón — algodão

A q-tip is made of cotton.

conditions

conditions

conditions

condiciones

condições

What are the weather conditions.

---

bell

cloche

cloche

campana

Sino

I hear the bell ringing!

---

apple

pomme

Pomme

manzana

maçã

Apples are a popular fruit.

children   les enfants

les enfants

niños   crianças

The children are playing.

---

nest   nid

nid

nido   ninho

The bird has a nest.

---

column   colonne

colonne

columna   coluna

Did you read the newspaper column?

shoe   chaussure

chaussure

zapato   sapato

I have new shoes.

Greek   grec

grec

griego   grego

Have you ever had Greek food?

France   france

France

francia   França

Have you ever been to France?

street

rue

rue

calle

rua

They walk across the street.

---

page

page

page

página

página

Please turn the page.

---

ring

bague

bague

anillo

anel

The bird is holding a ring.

cow   vache

vache

vaca   vaca

The cow is standing up.

---

watch   l'horloge

l'horloge

reloj   relógio

My watch is ticking.

---

seed   la graine

la graine

semilla   semente

We will plant the seeds.

fresh   frais

Frais

fresco   fresco

All the fruit is fresh.

example   exemple

exemple

ejemplo   exemplo

This is an example of a bird.

cat   chat

chat

gato   gato

That cat is adorable.

toy   jouet

jouet

juguete   brinquedo

He has a whole box of toys.

---

egg   oeuf

Oeuf

huevo   ovo

The bunny has many eggs.

---

coat   manteau

manteau

saco   casaco

She is wearing her coat.

boat | bateau

bateau

barco | barco

The boat is sailing.

---

eye | œil

œil

ojo | olho

He is closing his eyes.

---

four | quatre

quatre

cuatro | quatro

There were four of them.

pig

porc

porc

cerdo

porco

She is lying on the pig.

---

company

compagnie

compagnie

empresa

companhia

What company do you work for?

---

rain

pluie

pluie

lluvia

chuva

We love the rain!

dog   chien

chien

perro   cão

The dog wants to eat sweets.

oxygen   oxygène

oxygène

oxígeno   oxigênio

What is the symbol for oxygen?

rope   corde

corde

cuerda   corda

Do you have any rope?

morning   matin

Matin

mañana   manhã

I wake up in the morning.

office   bureau

Bureau

oficina   escritório

Do you need any office supplies?

fish   poisson

poisson

pez   peixe

There are two fish.

chicken

poulet

poulet

pollo

frango

The chicken is laying eggs.

paper

papier

papier

papel

papel

I like to color on paper.

bed

lit

lit

cama

cama

We all share three beds.

school · école

école

colegio · escola

They are going to school.

---

snow · neige

neige

nieve · neve

I have fun in the snow.

---

leg · jambe

jambe

pierna · perna

My leg is feeling better.

bear — ours

ours

oso — Urso

The bear likes to eat honey.

---

game — jeu

Jeu

juegos — jogos

What game is it?

---

picture — image

image

imagen — cenário

He is taking some pictures.

father   père

père

papá   Papai

He is a nice father.

---

time   temps

temps

hora   Tempo

He is telling the time.

---

robin   robin

Robin

robin   robin

The robin is helping Santa.

day

journée

journée

día

dia

Month
30

This day is the 30th.

---

horse

cheval

cheval

cheval

caballo

cavalo

The horse is galloping.

---

face

visage

visage

visage

cara

cara

They were at the face painting booth.

song   chanson

chanson

canciones   músicas

She is singing a song.

---

wind   vent

vent

viento   vento

The wind blows the leaves.

---

flower   fleur

fleur

flor   flor

She is holding a flower.

grass · herbe

herbe

césped · Relva

The goat is eating the grass.

---

birthday · anniversaire

anniversaire

cumpleaños · aniversário

Today is my birthday.

---

kitty · minou

minou

gatito · gatinha

I like my kitty.

door   porte

porte

puerta   porta

He is knocking on the door.

---

baby   bébé

bébé

bebé   bebê

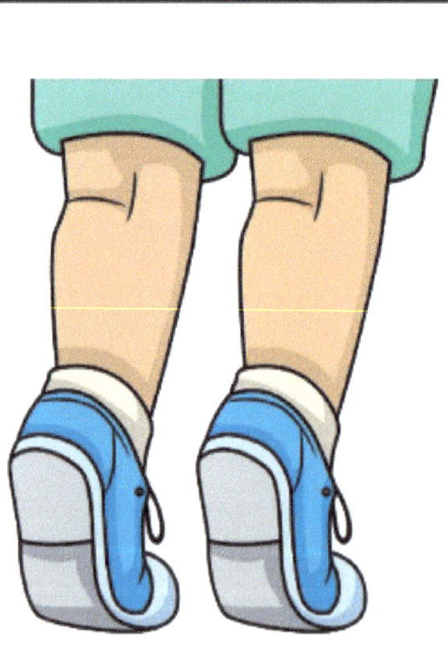

The baby is crawling.

---

feet   pieds

pieds

pies   pés

His feet are swollen.

doll   poupée

poupée

muñeca   boneca

She is hugging her doll.

cake   gâteau

gâteau

pastel   bolo

The cake is white and pink.

farmer   fermier

fermier

agricultor   agricultor

The farmer had a farm.

jardin

They are going to the garden.

fête

I love to go to parties.

arbre

She is sitting under a tree.

top

haut

Haut

tapas

topo

We like to play with tops.

---

mother

mère

mère

madre

mãe

My mother loves me.

---

score

but

But

puntuación

Ponto

What was the final score?

sheep mouton

mouton

oveja ovelha

The sheep have fluffy wool.

---

ball balle

Balle

pelota bola

He is bouncing the ball.

---

head tête

tête

cabeza cabeça

She has a hat on her head.

squirrel   écureuil

écureuil

ardilla   esquilo

The squirrel is on the tree.

---

rose   rose

Rose

rosa   rosa

Thank you for the rose.

---

milk   lait

Lait

leche   leite

The baby is drinking milk.

brother   frère

frère

hermano   irmão

They are brothers.

box   boîte

boîte

caja   caixa

The box is full of clothes.

night   nuit

nuit

noche   noite

We sleep at night.

ground   sol

sol

suelo   terra

It plays a trick on the ground.

---

wood   bois

bois

madera   madeira

He plays with wooden blocks

---

home   maison

maison

casa   casa

He drew a picture of his home.

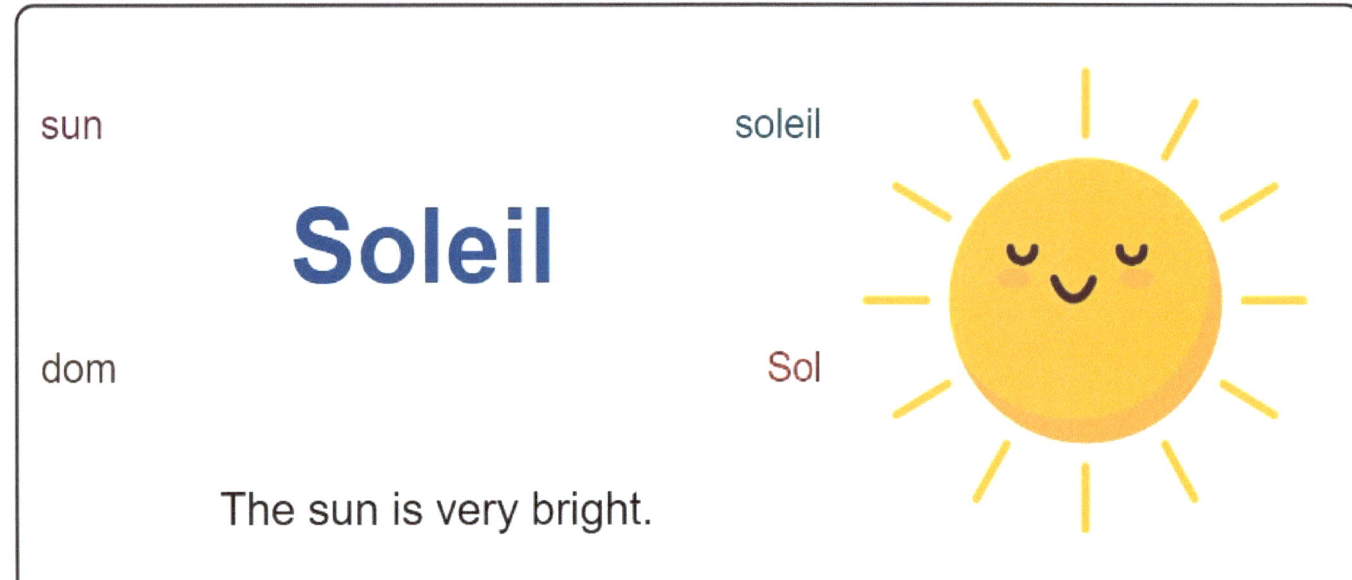

sun

soleil

Soleil

dom

Sol

The sun is very bright.

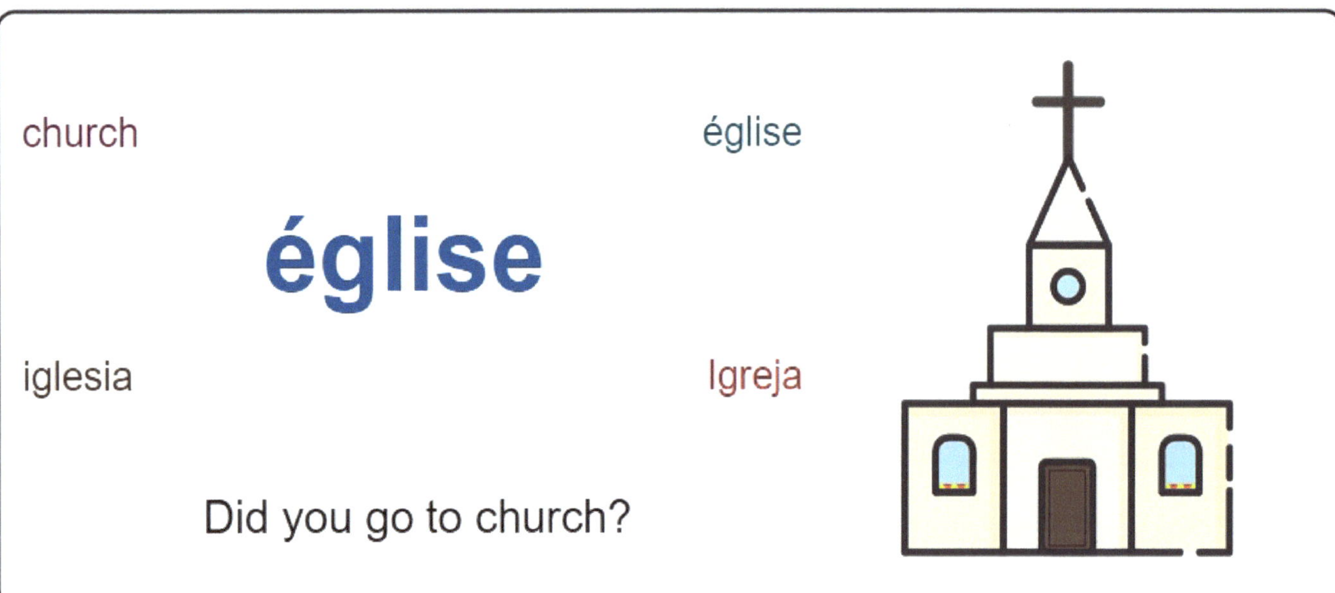

church

église

église

iglesia

Igreja

Did you go to church?

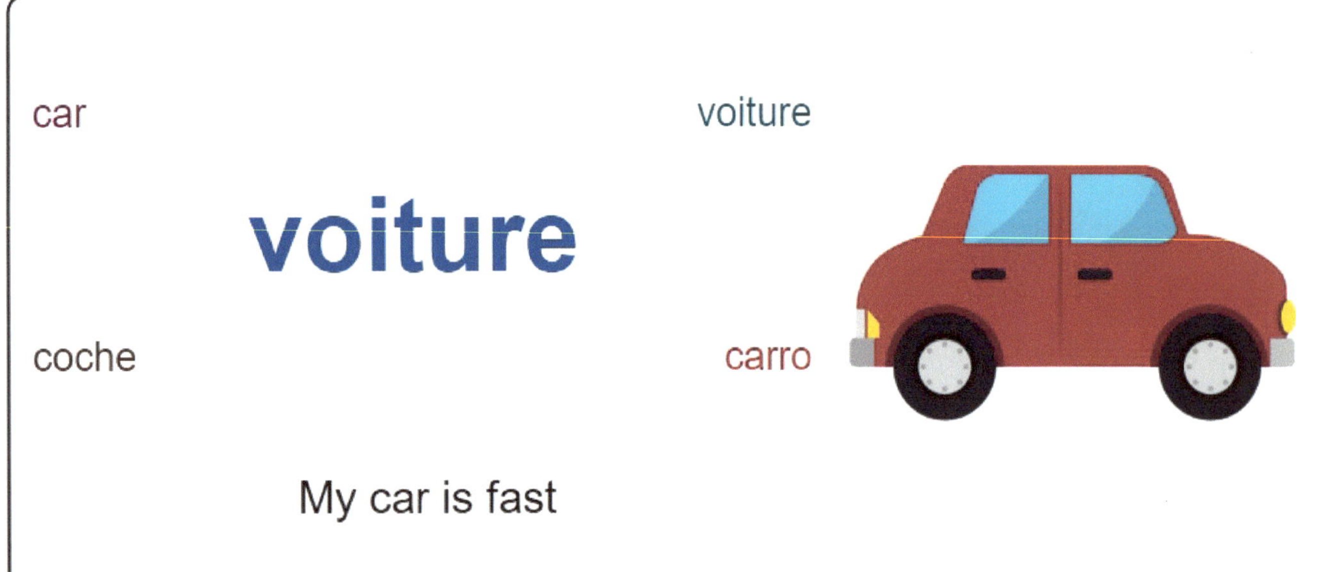

car

voiture

voiture

coche

carro

My car is fast

way façon

façon

camino caminho

They find a way back home.

name nom

Nom

nombre nome

My name is Joe.

place endroit

endroit

sitio locais

This is my favorite place.

farm   ferme

ferme

granja   Fazenda

The farm has lots of animals.

---

goodbye   au revoir

Au revoir

adiós   Tchau

The bear is saying goodbye.

---

hand   main

main

mano   mão

You should wash your hands.

family

famille

familia

famille

famille

família

How big is your family?

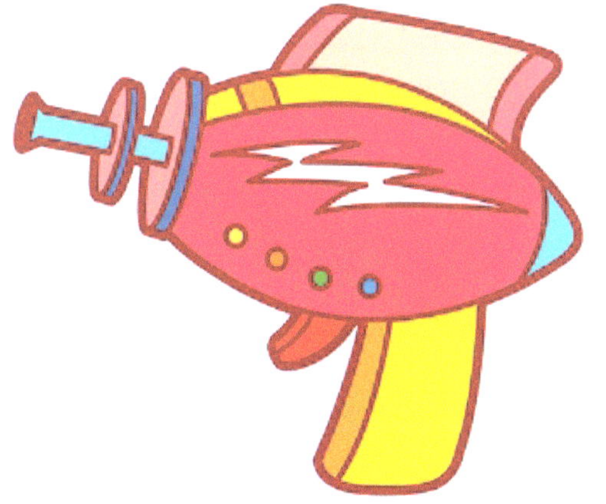

gun

pistolet

pistola

armas

pistolet

pistolet

We played with a water gun.

window

fenêtre

ventana

janela

fenêtre

fenêtre

The window is open.

water — l'eau

l'eau

agua — água

He is drinking water.

---

bread — pain

pain

un pan — pão

She is baking some bread.

---

sister — sœur

sœur

hermana — irmã

She is my sister.

seat   siège

siège

asiento   assento

The girls took a seat in the sand.

---

chart   graphique

graphique

gráfico   gráfico

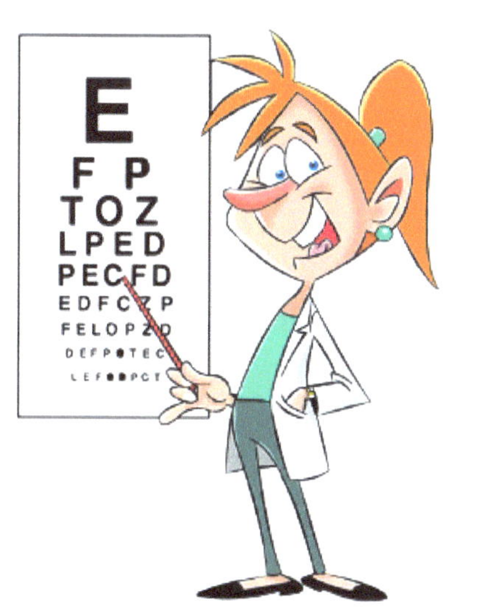

What does your medical chart say?

---

children   les enfants

les enfants

niños   crianças

Four children sang.

food   aliments

aliments

comida   Comida

They made a lot of food.

---

city   ville

ville

ciudad   cidade

He worked in the city.

---

boy   garçon

garçon

chico   Garoto

The boy is eating dinner.

hill

colline

colline

colina

Colina

The house is on the hill.

---

nose

nez

nez

nariz

nariz

My nose is running.

---

corn

blé

blé

maíz

milho

I grow corn in the garden.

letter   alphabet

alphabet

alfabeto   alfabeto

Learn English letters is fun.

---

thing   chose

chose

cosa   coisa

I am thinking of many things.

---

money   argent

argent

dinero   dinheiro

I save money in my piggy bank.

men

hommes

Hommes

hombres

homens

The men are arguing.

---

table

table

table

mesa

mesa

There is a toy on the table.

---

chair

chaises

chaises

sillas

cadeiras

He is sitting on the chair.

rabbit   lapin

lapin

conejo   Coelho

The rabbit wants to play.

bird   oiseau

oiseau

pájaro   pássaro

The bird is dancing happily.

duck   canard

canard

pato   Pato

The duck is swimming.

man | homme

homme

hombre | cara

This man is my dad.

---

fire | feu

Feu

fuego | fogo

Fire is hot.

---

stick | bâton

bâton

palo | bastão

He is playing sticks.